A TALE OF FOREVERLAND

A TALE OF
FOREVERLAND

CAROLYN NYSTROM
Illustrated by Janice Skivington

INTERVARSITY PRESS
DOWNERS GROVE, ILLINOIS 60515

Originally published in HIS Magazine, April 1977.

InterVarsity Press is the book-publishing division of InterVarsity Christian Fellowship, a student movement active on campus at hundreds of universities, colleges and schools of nursing in the United States of America, and a member movement of the International Fellowship of Evangelical Students. For information about local and regional activities, write Public Relations Dept., InterVarsity Christian Fellowship, 6400 Schroeder Rd., P.O. Box 7895, Madison, WI 53707-7895.

Cover illustration: Janice Skivington

ISBN 0-8308-1840-5

Printed in Mexico ∞

Library of Congress Cataloging-in-Publication Data

Nystrom, Carolyn.
    A tale of foreverland: a story for old and young/by Carolyn
Nystrom: illustrated by Janice Skivington.
        p.   cm.
    "Originally published in His magazine"—T.p. verso.
    ISBN 0-8308-1840-5
    1. Consolation.   I. Title.
    BV4905.2.N97   1992
    242—dc20   92-12355
                                                                CIP

15	14	13	12	11	10	9	8	7	6	5	4	3	2	1
04	03	02	01	00	99	98	97	96	95	94	93	92		

"THE TIME IS COME!"
"COME, COME!"

The cry was faint, first beginning high among the peaks of Piris and Satoris. But as the water tumbling from the slopes gained momentum and became a gurgling, rushing, jubilant torrent, so the cry echoed and bounced from peak to peak, then gained intensity and joy as it reached toward the lush valley below.

"Come, come!"

"The time is come!"

From the hollows and peaks and valleys and forests responded those who heard the call. Their feet fairly danced along the paths and through the meadows. Children skipped hand in hand. A teenage girl carried a young baby. The old traveled as swiftly as the young, for their age showed in wisdom of face not in feebleness of body. Their voices were joyous. Some who had traveled this path before led the way while others to whom it was new followed excitedly in their wake.

S o o n   a   s o n g   b e g a n ,
a simple melody, perhaps started by a child.
Others joined and the melody repeated itself first
high and then low and then all tones in between.
The tune became as convoluted as the sparkling
stream, almost turning back upon itself, then
reaching out in a new adventurous direction.
Each member of the throng sang his own ver-
sion yet blended perfectly with the rest. The song
was one of praise but the words were heard by
Him alone. Only the magic of the music reached
the ears of the singers, for even they could not
bear to know the strength of their combined
words.

Still the cry was heard reaching into the most
hidden of fertile valleys:

"The time is come."

"Come, come!"

"The time is come!"

Philip worked his skillful
fingers through the loose rich soil. The pure air held the scent of warm moist dirt mixed with the cool aroma of the woodland nearby. He straightened his back, long bent over seedling plants.

He had been working on a new strain of the *Diapensia lapponica.* Its flower was dainty and perfect, and it pleased Philip to be creating beauty together with Him. He stretched his muscular back with satisfied tiredness. Then he listened eagerly to the cry.

"Come, come!"

It was a familiar call to Philip, yet it never failed to bring a surge of anticipation in him. The cry was heard only by those for whom it was intended, and it had been intended many times for him. That was one of the advantages of coming here at an early age.

He laid his tools aside and moved toward the growing throng and the borning chamber.

The borning chamber was
a place of birth, of new life, but also a place of shadows as Philip knew well. It was the only link to the place of time, and the glimpse it afforded into that other domain was often disquieting. For this reason only one, the one closest to the child being born, would actually enter the borning chamber and assist with the birth.

Philip's first experience in this place had occurred shortly after his own trip. He had been called to the chamber to welcome his younger brother, Tommy. Tommy, with the easy trust of a five-year-old who knew that what Mommy had told him was true, came confident and unafraid.

He had quickly placed his hand in Philip's and asked to be taken to Him. It was Philip who, after that quick glimpse into the place of time, needed the reassurance and comfort that only He was able to supply.

There had been other calls since. Often he had waited outside the chamber and been part of the hugs and kisses of the joyous welcome to the new arrival. Sometimes he entered alone and emerged triumphant with the new guest. Once he had met his college buddy, Rod, and then Uncle Wade, and later a tiny baby niece was in his arms. With each trip into the borning chamber his fear of what he saw in the other world decreased, and he was left with only a desire to make the trip enjoyable for the one to whom he ministered.

Philip's stride lengthened

as he joined the crowd, now quite large. He fell into step beside Letha, who bounced her crowing young niece. Sometimes it was possible to discover who was being born by noting those who had been called to welcome the birth. Only those who had known the new arrival in the place of time would be called. Surveying the faces, he surmised that the person probably had lived long in that other world—and that it might be a member of his family since Tommy and Uncle Wade were both present. But there were many others waiting whom he did not know—this new guest must have brought many to Him.

He lifted his voice and joined in the wordless song of praise. And he felt the deep thrust of joy within him that the song never failed to produce. Soon the song shifted to a joyous exuberant chant:

"The time is come!"

"The time is come!"

"The time is come!"—each phrase rising and falling on the other as it expressed the inner delight of every person preparing to receive into this perfect place the one about to be born.

The borning chamber was
a low earthen structure extending into the ground. The chant became subdued as each one in the crowd listened for the call from within. Philip too quieted his voice, intent on the invitation about to be issued.

"The time is come!

Come, come.

The time is come.

Come, come, come, come."

Once again he had been chosen to minister to the one about to be born. Philip stooped to pass through the entrance.

Inside was a long dark narrow passage on a steep slant with a window at each end. Philip turned his back on the one, knowing that it opened toward Piris, the highest peak of his world. The other, mist-covered, was at the bottom of the chamber and angled so sharply that it was almost as much a part of the floor as of the wall.

Philip walked steadily down toward this lower window. He squared his shoulders as though to draw a little extra strength and bent his frame to the task before him. As he approached the window the mist cleared so that just in front of him, almost at arm's length, was the scene to which he had been called.

He found himself peering into a hospital room. He could feel the tension in the figures there present. Two white-clad nurses scurried about adjusting valves, timing intravenous drips, while a doctor bent over the bed, stethoscope moving quickly as he listened. A middle-aged woman sat uncomfortably nearby as if trying to keep out of the way yet needing to be near. The doctor moved away from the bed and stood beside her chair. He placed a hand on her shoulder and whispered sadly and helplessly, "The time is come."

Philip looked at the figure on the bed before him. It was wrinkled, thin and old but he recognized it. Now he knew why he had been called. The eyes gazing back at him were his mother's.

He remembered his own trip through this narrow passage. It had been unexpected. He was a young man of nineteen, a college freshman intent on an engineering career. He was just beginning to search his mind for a basis for his faith. He suspected that parental conditioning was insufficient reason for belief in a God who loves man, hates sin, grants salvation, desires worship and prepares life hereafter.

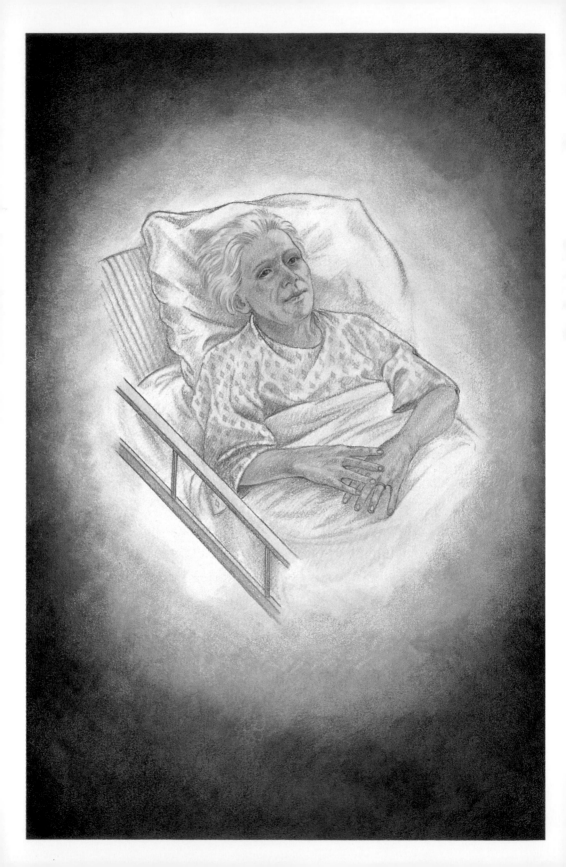

Would his boyhood faith

have survived the questions he was ready to ask —would it have deepened and matured? Philip didn't know. A raging attack of meningitis came, and within hours (by measure of the place of time) he was dragged clinging, choking and crying to this place. He hadn't even dared open his eyes to see the fearful world to which he was being transported.

But the eyes that met his now were unafraid, displaying his mother's trust—the same trust she had given Tommy. They were also filled with pain, and he longed to quiet it for her. He beckoned to her and could see the longing in her expression.

"Come, come," he whispered softly. "The time is come. Come, He calls."

Still, pain wrenched her body and refused to release her from its clutches.

Philip knew that some token of the future might relieve her agony He whispered. "Let me show you. I will move away for just a moment. You must look through the window. Then I'll return."

"See?" he gestured behind him.

He stood aside briefly so that she could see the mountain peaks beyond the chamber. As he returned to his post he was rewarded by a weak smile, and her lips moved to say, "Thank you."

Eagerly he waited, sometimes speaking softly to her, comforting when the pain tore her, waiting, reaching toward her, watching as her breathing slowed, as her color faded, as the nurses retreated now to the seated woman. Philip watched their sorrow yet did not share it, for he stood apart from this place of time.

As their sadness deepened, his anticipation increased.

Then the window again misted and suddenly she was with him. Her arms were strong around his neck, her breathing solid, her voice sure.

"My son! My Philip! How I've missed you!"

"Come, Mom, let me show you."

Hand in hand, up the steep passage they climbed toward the window. They stopped to drink in the view. He pointed out Piris and Satoris and Androma, and far beyond the outline of Rajeks. They talked of the old world and the new, of their love for Him and His love for them.

Sometimes they laughed as they shared each other's worlds. Sometimes they held each other close. It may have been hours or days. No matter.

When she was ready Philip again took her hand. "Come, Mom. You've got quite a welcoming party gathered for your birth."

Arm in arm they emerged
from the borning chamber, and a cheer burst from the crowd.

"The time is come!"

"Now time is no more!"

"Time no more!" they shouted to her. They engulfed her with greetings.

Her brother Wade kissed her cheek.

A pastor from her childhood shook her hand again.

A young woman Philip didn't know said, "Sara, you showed me how to get here, but I came first."

Tommy caught her around the waist with a little-boy hug. "I knew you'd come. You said you would."

Letha deposited her gurgling granddaughter into her arms. She laughed and hugged them all until she was breathless with happiness. Then, the baby still in arm, she turned to Philip.

"I must see Him. Please take me to Him."

"Yes, we will go to Him. Then I'll show you my work. There's this new *Diapensia lapponica.* . . ."

He will wipe away every tear from their eyes,
and death shall be no more,
neither shall there be mourning
nor crying nor pain any more,
for the former things have passed away.
Revelation 21:4

This edition of *A Tale of Foreverland* is set in 12 point Leawood and printed on 80# Patina Matte by R. R. Donnelley & Sons Co., Reynosa/McAllen Division. Color separations are by Computer Color Graphics, Inc. of Hillside, Illinois.